GIVEN

WINNER OF THE 2022 AUTUMN HOUSE RISING WRITER PRIZE

given

poems

liza katz duncan

AUTUMN
HOUSE PRESS

Library of Congress Cataloging-in-Publication Data
Names: Duncan, Liza Katz, author.
Title: Given : poems / Liza Katz Duncan.
Description: Pittsburgh, PA : Autumn House Press, [2022]
Identifiers: LCCN 2022044280 (print) | LCCN 2022044281 (ebook) | ISBN
  9781637680681 (paperback) | ISBN 9781637680698 (epub)
Subjects: LCGFT: Poetry.
Classification: LCC PS3604.U5288 G58 2022 (print) | LCC PS3604.U5288
  (ebook) | DDC 811/.6--dc23/eng/20220913
LC record available at https://lccn.loc.gov/2022044280
LC ebook record available at https://lccn.loc.gov/20220442
  Printed in the United States on acid-free paper that meets the inter-
national standards of permanent books intended for purchase by libraries.

Autumn House Press is a nonprofit corporation whose mission is the publication and
promotion of poetry and other fine literature. The press gratefully acknowledges support
from individual donors, public and private foundations, and government agencies. This
book was supported, in part, by the Greater Pittsburgh Arts Council through its Allegheny
Arts Revival Grant and the Pennsylvania Council on the Arts, a state agency funded by
the Commonwealth of Pennsylvania. This project is supported, in part, by the National
Endowment for the Arts. To find out more about how National Endowment for the
Arts grants impact individuals and communities, visit www.arts.gov.

Cover and Book Design by Joel W. Coggins

FOR CHRIS

I've read that the ocean

is a large pot of Apocalypse soup soon to boil over with our sins

NATALIE DIAZ

The tide rewrites a place. Whatever the tide brings, it displaces what could have been, submerges what once was.

NICOLA SEBASTIAN

CONTENTS

I

II

III

GIVEN

I

BAYSHORE ELEGY

Cars hiss on the wet streets. Rain dissipates the smell
of low tide, dried seaweed. The bay
spits up a tire swing: sunsick rubber, split rope.

You'd have to be crazy to call home
a strip of sand that will be underwater
in fifty years and oh,

my God, what does that make me?
Before slag and smelt and lead, this was clam country.
Then, during Prohibition, a causeway for bootleg,
the bottles dumped overboard at the sight of police.

Even now, barefoot, you might cut your feet
on hundred-year-old glass the bay purged.
I lean against the window, listen

for another rush of rain. I shouldn't
be here: I've come home
the way rain returns to the earth only
to become runoff, to take with it whatever it can carry.

But don't misunderstand: I'll carry this
when the bay takes it all back. Call of the grackle,
whine of the turkey vulture. Blighted clams,

raw and red in their half shells.
The harbor, insistent where it shifts against the gravel,
where turning cars leave, in their wake, infinity signs.

EKPHRASIS: SANDY

In the Weather Underground photos, it appears
no more than an optical illusion: look at it this way,
it's an eagle's crest; that way, a snail shell. A trick
of the light, or of the mind.
                              The sky makes and remakes.
Trees reach sideways: hear us. Under cloud cover,
behind caution tape, a town the bay built and unbuilt.

A Volvo, shipwrecked.
Three hunched figures in black
row a lifeboat down Central Ave.

In the blurred background, a Wawa.
The sign still bears the old logo.
Three-layered sun: lemon, saffron,
bittersweet. A single goose in flight.

Half a carousel, a balancing act. The dragon
three feet away, less fearsome out of context.
An organ's phantom cipher. Bright centerpiece.

A daylight moon, bloated over the bay,
pulls the tide high over the bulkhead
the way one might lift a child, their small fingers
struggling. See where the water left
prints of yellow foam for days.

As if filtered through a smoke screen, a haze of sky,
its diaphanous glaze. A street sign flails, flag-like.

One woman holds an umbrella inside out, like a wounded bird.
She's carrying coupons, grocery bags, a sweater.

The girl in the blurred part of the photo is smiling.
But then, *children see adventure in disruption.*

See the foam blow through her hair,

                    sand on her tongue. Her sense of time

                stretches only the length of this boardwalk,
                  where the ocean leaps onto the planks.

                  Only foam now, but soon it will swallow
                   everything in the photo's frame. See,

             in the grain of the wood, where it's already happened:
               a green stain, cyclone-shaped, spreading.

A picture taken through a window, the frame
crowded as the last ferry out of town.
Oil rainbows, gray cumulus smoke,
phone tower silhouettes, bayside factories.
Debris superimposed in the foreground,
as if to justify yet another skyline shot.
The flashbulb blotting out the tiny sun.

GIVEN

Given a factory town, smokestacks that leaked poison into the bay until it swelled, glowed green, too liquid for its frame

Given the sky breaks and remakes, pours its wet rage on the tortured apartments. Even the manor on the hill, that stronghold, shaken, foundation rolling like the planet itself

Given the smell of machine tinged with singed fist of hair, the hiss and spit of ash

Given the water, as seen from the road, is already at eye level

Given the lights have dulled the constellations from the skies

Given the blackjack oak, bare branches pitchforking skyward

Given the blighted tissue of leaves; the wind, a graceless pallbearer

Given the cell tower's obelisk

Given clams turned to plastic in their shells

Given once, this was a harbor

Given chemical clouds stipple the sky—

BOXWOODS

We didn't tokenize our grief with candles
or crosses. Harbored no belief in ghosts,
though we wondered about movements in the boxwoods,

the horses' sudden startles, the dim flickers,
inexplicable, years later, in the house.

Wondered what the moths that scaled the walls,
groped the windowpanes for solace,
were hiding. The dead are territorial;

this we understood. We knew why mothers
named their daughters after things that cling

to the ground: so many Rosemarys and Ivys,
Hazels and Lavenders begging to be buried,
the scent of boxwoods sticking to their skin.

APOSTROPHE

Ocean, every so often, a kitchen tile or child's toy
rises from you, years after the hurricane's passed.

This time, the disaster was somewhere else.
The disaster was always somewhere else, until it wasn't.

Punctuation of the morning after: comma between
red sky and sailors' warning, white space where a storm cloud lowers.

Where the bay breaks away, the sentence ends: a waning
crescent of peninsula, barely visible

but for the broken buildings, the ambulance lights.
Ocean, even now, even shaken, you hold the memory

of words, of worlds that failed slowly, then all at once.
A flotilla of gulls falls onto you, mourners draped in slate.

GIVEN

Can't he see that our bodies
are just our bodies, tied to what we know?
   —Patricia Smith

Given the urgency with which humans run toward water, have always run toward water

Given the human impulse to build at the tide's fingertips

Given ancient civilizations evolved on floodplains, thrived for thousands of years, and there are those who flourish still: who don't hold onto trappings, or have none to hold onto, who fold their dark tents onto their backs once a year and walk to higher ground

Given *our bodies are just our bodies*, 78 percent water

Given my neighbor Rebecca, who had nowhere to go; who hadn't packed, was wearing all her valuables when the storm hit

Given the wedding ring from a previous marriage, the bruise it made on her swollen finger a parenthesis left open

Given this house and everything in it is everything she's ever made or done: an oil painting of a fisherman at high tide. A clam shell for an ashtray. Five rooms. One life

Given all of these floating through the flooded house like driftwood

Given the basement filled like a bathtub

Given roads turned to rivers

Given bodies fished from the phragmites

Given a growing ocean

What else could she have done?

THE UNCLES

One served in the navy. Another's son lived at home,
about my age. One used to watch the birds.
One was a carpenter and built the fence
that ran the length of the beach, ending where land
met water. They'd share a bottle, stare at the bay,
talking tides, the catch, and people they knew.

One called me the professor. I never really knew
why. After working late one night I came home,
found him reminiscing. How they'd jump into the bay
as boys, off the old bridge. Half-men, half-birds,
that three-second flicker in midair before landing.
The new bridge: a colossus with a ten-foot suicide fence.

(Years later, someone whispered across the fence
that the son my age had died that way.) They knew
the tides like some know train schedules, knew the land
without a map, and by flood stains on the homes
could catalog storms by name. They recognized birds
by their calls, recognized boys who'd drowned in the bay

years earlier. It happens, living near the bay
your whole life, said the carpenter, who'd built the fence.
Inevitable, said the one who watched the birds.
They'd seen entire towns subsumed on the news,
the rubble of oceanfront camelots. Seen homes
fray and crumple, seen neighbors head inland,

leaving the keys in the door. Their faces creased, hands
calloused from years of fishing in the bay.
This was their home to claim, not mine. Home
to them was a dead end and a guardrail or fence,

then water.

 I'm forgetting others, I know.
One had a scar near his eye in the shape of a bird.

One, a firefighter, had tattooed the word
mercy, and fed the feral cats. When the land-
lord asked, no one would ever say who.
It doesn't matter now. When I drive past the bay
I remember, though the scene's changed: old homes
tilted on their axes. The harbor, dark. The fence,

fallen. The people they knew, gone. Even birds
won't land here. The uncles have moved to retirement homes,
fenced in, built as far as possible from the bay.

WAWA POEM

No matter where you go in this town, water

is always within walking distance. Every street
a testament: *You cannot remove water from water.*

On the Wawa convenience store sign
the Canada goose always flies toward water,

its back aligned with the *W*'s twin serifs.
The name itself, the first syllable of water,

a start and restart, a hesitation, as if by speaking
the word in full, you might conjure water

where you least want it. Look: some saltwater

bird has built its nest in the second *a* of the sign,
its round acrylic mouth as hospitable as any watery

cliff or sand dune. The *a* invites life; the *w*
sloughs it off: the name, when written, like water.

At high tide, we get our coffees to go
and walk down to the bay. The sound of water

against the seawall, brash and arrhythmic,
as if something underwater

is arching, is aching, to come up for air.

GIVEN

Given a liquor store boarded up with plywood left over from Irene
        spray-painted *No Booze for Sandy*

Given shelves already scoured
        in the mad tumble before the storm

Given no power, no transportation

Given the storm thickened on them
        and day by day she taught them how to drink, to chase
        sickness with ocean

Given the empties, an array of colors like so many boardwalk sno-cones,
        and how they drank, thirsty children all

Given the storm stayed for days,
        crawling into bed with them, nursing them to sleep

Given they drank to disappear a brew of rainwater,
        liquor, and ocean: where else
        was all that liquid going to go

Given a gasoline river burned in the streets,
        singeing even their eyelashes

Given No Outlet signs knee-deep

Given all the time in the world
        and little use for alarm

I WANTED TO BE SURROUNDED BY WATER

Tonight, at the end of the hottest summer on record,

after three consecutive record-breaking summers,
my husband and his brother are hooking up the gas generator,

dragging the porch furniture into the shed.

There's a tropical storm watch along the Jersey Shore
and people are bracing themselves for evacuation.

Some people don't choose this. I did—

I wanted to be surrounded by water. To find home
easily on a map. I wanted streets with names

that were self-explanatory: Harbor Way. Shore Concourse.

I wanted to mark, on the shoreline,
their disappearance—the way,

at the site of an accident near Highway 35, someone

hung crosses, plastic flowers, photos of a young girl—
I wanted, also, to leave something behind.

To document what was, and what will never be—

I wanted the thick promise of soil, wanted
to expect recklessly. I wanted to sit still

enough that something could take root under me.

I wanted to greet migrating birds from an off-season
beach as empty as I was, waiting

for the ocean's sharp punctuation. I wanted an August

raucous with crickets, katydids,
creatures I didn't even know how to see, creatures

making new creatures despite everything, so unfailingly alive.

I wanted my children to ride their bikes to the end of the road,
climb over the guardrail and watch New York gleam across the bay—

and when it rained, I wanted them to look up

at the same lightning-pocked
sky I'd seen—

I wanted children, despite the dying world.

In my husband's box of old papers, a journal entry
from the flood of '92. They slept on cots in a school cafeteria

for days, waited in the dark.

Then, the bay receded. Those who still had homes went back.
If you live here long enough, you'll know

this is just part of living.

But there are more storms now, more floods.
More and more people leave.

I wanted, also, to leave this place behind.

I moved to Boston, where I had no ties, made no sense
while two storms, one after the other, pummeled

everyone I knew back home. Even now,

the high-water mark signs, Irene and Sandy,
link arms like two sisters standing on the shore.

Even now, scars on the buildings from the swilling ocean—

from the flames and ashes, the slow and quiet smoke.
All this to say: I wasn't here, not when it mattered most.

What mattered most:

There were some who rode the storm out
   on the porch, waited for waves

to gather, then crest over the bulkhead—fog
   was the shabbiest color, known

by its smell of salt, outside those houses
   where they'd learned to feel

the tightening of a hasp reverberate
   in their chests, how the wind

forked every birch that bent at the waist,
   tore the pear tree's husk

from its stake, unclustered elderberry,
   elderflower. Some things break

at the first sign of decay: a canoe,
   poisoned oysters in the bay, sinews

from some other, storm-slaught
   house: its plumbing, kitchen tiles,

shingles laced with tarp. In the driveway,
   a boat trailer harvesting rust—

I wanted children, despite
the dying world.

Say what you will: expectation softened

the impact of a hundred-year flood,
softened even the atramental rain,

which softened the earth to our shoes.

The child we lost—a girl I don't know.
She occurs to me in photographic shades: ochre,

burnt sienna, vintage bronze. Memory

has softened her outline, as the bay
smooths edges of broken glass,

returning it graspable,

shatterproof. In the haze
of the neon sky, flecks of her face

flash in and out of focus.

Say what you will; this is home now.
I walk these beaches. I lost a child here.

I had to write myself back into this place, if only to watch it

fall apart. But tonight—
tonight the storm turns quietly in on itself.

No one evacuates. Only a few tree limbs on the lawn,

and a silver pulse of sky.
My husband and I drive to the bay to see

the benign clouds, the sun sinking over the factories.

We watch the leaves turn inside out: a storm warning
come too late. The bay rising so softly we barely notice.

To document what was, and what will never be—

At a writers' conference the following spring, a poet who had never been to the Jersey Shore read her award-winning piece inspired by a photo, now iconic, of a roller coaster Sandy had submerged. Maybe you know it: it was the Jet Star roller coaster, the one that fell off the end of Casino Pier in Seaside Heights. "Such a cool image," the poet said.

I wanted to hate that poem. To think I was better than that. I wanted, at least, to think my poems were better than that, though they weren't, not even close. It was actually a pretty good poem. That was the worst part about it.

I wanted to ask the poet if it had occurred to her that this "cool image" wasn't hers to use, that to call it an image at all was insulting, as if there were anything figurative about it. I wanted to ask her why something beautiful had to be destroyed in order for her to see it, though I hadn't seen it myself, either.

And when I finally did see it, from a shattered boardwalk like the one where my grandfather had bagged groceries during the Depression, where my mother had ridden her bike as a child, I wanted to think I was more than a disaster tourist. I wanted to make something braver of that wreck than everyone else who had stood on the boardwalk that day, looking only at their cameras, their faces distorted in the tidepool's funhouse mirror. I wanted to know enough to write the poems I most wanted—or needed—to hear. (I will never know enough.)

I wanted so much, and thought I deserved it. Who the fuck did I think I was?

I wanted, mostly, to be brave enough to rename myself after something tangible. To say, *Here is my life. Here is everything I am.*

II

RETROSPECT

Years laced with gauze, with bias cuts and paper cuts,

fringed dresses, singed fingers. Layered like macadam,

onion and ocean, paint and plaster and earth. Armorless

she clamored toward the door, down steps steep and slick

that disappeared in twos, then threes; between leaping

and landing shame-soaked, snakebite-swollen: this is how

she learned to scream. Years like photos taken inside a handbag,

gray and accidental, reeking of mace. No longer

the girl wishing to be older, who

smokes between classes, perfects a poker face.

She won't be disappointed. In false lighting the room

spins planetary: a world enamored, tinged with the promise

of a poison pill or miracle berry. A world that craves

a glimpse, wants her guardless, a world that insists.

KRISTINA

Nothing for her here, in the dark house.
        Nothing outside but grocery lines,

gas lines. The bay under an ice floe;
        below, waves suspended mid-curl.

Only an interruption of snow to discern
        land from water. Across it, Brooklyn fades.

In the blurred dark she fingers her ribs
        like piano keys, runs one fingernail

down the crease at the corner of her mouth
        to measure out the years.

In five days she hasn't
        left the house, but she wants

the snow-bright world outside her window.
        She wants it desperately. She wants it

not at all. If I don't make it out tonight, she thinks,
        it will not be a tragedy: or if it is, it will be

a small one, compared to those outside:
        the crocus, snow-drenched, rotted before bloom;

the nest of stray cats taken by the frost;
        the neighbors' houses, flooded, boarded up.

It's the fifth night, the twenty-second drink.
        On the bay, the full Wolf Moon's misleading path.

She dreams of factory clouds,
      a chemical haze, poisoned oysters

in a milk-thick bay. The dream-sky
      pelts her with geometric snow,

its angular moon a code
      her iPhone could demystify.

Behind the dream-house, the dream-trees wake,
      shake away white shawls, and she rises with them.

Sky, she says, I'd get on my knees
      before you: for clean water, for birds'

neat chevrons, for constellations.
      If I thought I could move you to tears—

Outside, wind picks the bones of the frailest trees.
      She dresses in the dark. The daughter

has put herself to bed again, closed the door to keep
      the monsters out. Seeing this, her heart cracks open.

She's shared homes with monsters.
      Doors don't stop their ebbs and fluxes

from a darkened hallway to a restless mind;
      they enter quietly, as floodwaters seep

through fault lines in the plaster. Even
　　　　at daybreak, they peer through the curtains.

Leave vestiges of themselves in an illness,
　　　　a bad habit. The daughter

is eight years old, and already monsters
　　　　have touched down, have laid their terrible eggs.

❧

Her daughter still asleep, she stands on the pier.
　　　　Once, a goat dove into a river, sprang a fish's tail.

In September's sky, you can see him
　　　　only faintly, but she understands: Even stars

bear horns. Even the sky holds monsters.
　　　　Effortless, to dive face-first into a bottle

or into the bay, and become a monster too. How easily
　　　　she could fall apart if given permission.

But she's forfeited that chance. A child's head against
　　　　her shoulder. The more it leaned, the more she had to hold.

Tonight, boats cut through the inlet.
　　　　The floodwaters finally recede. Gulls

cluster on temporary islands. Tomorrow, sodden furniture
　　　　to carry to the curb, sand to be swept from the porch.

GIVEN

Given January, an unseasonable warm front

Given fog covering most of the city

Given the ocean you try to swallow when you can no longer speak

Given the bottle you hold like it's a needle—like you could thread yourself through the eye if you could just make yourself small enough

Given your face when you drink alone, half-masked by blue light and the porch screen, mouth canyon-deep and narrow. Sweltering, a shell left open, beads of salt burgeoning on your skin

Given your Instagram photo, where you're six months sober and running on the beach

Given a photo is not a mirror

Given the bottle reflects only the bare trees

What did I expect—

that you'd emerge one day from the bottle like a genie, clean and eager to please?

INSTAGRAM PHOTO OF A WOMAN
FACING THE OCEAN

All the frustration comes up in the throat:
the roundness of *ocean*, guttural half-sound
of *chorus, apart*. What happens to girls who want
to be looked at, not looked through: wind
through the battens of their skeleton-boat,
this not-music, this ringing in the throat.

Mud-soaked hem, stained edge of a sleeve:
the perfect dress, sun off a whitewashed staircase,
though beautiful, overwhelms. We'll always have
this lack of symmetry: call it art, or avoidance,
the angles planned to help us not look *at her*—
the violence her reflection does to the water.

KRISTINA SPEAKS TO HER MOTHER

I've learned the language of your parables.

Some days I hear your voice inside my own, all panic grass and cautionary tales.

Today is like a painting. A flat sky, rough clouds reflected in the bay. Still, the water, ridged and solid, suggests something's off.

Below the surface, hundreds of Atlantic silverside. The color when they jump at once: shrill, shouldn't exist in nature.

The rotted remains of a dock, teeming with gulls and cormorants. Preening, already drunk on fish, they know when they've had their fill.

I hear your voice inside my own, your admonitions in the way I use the same word, carelessly, to mean two things. *Fish*: the creature, its displacement. *Drunk*: both person and past action.

Mother, if you could see what I've become. A Frankenstein (there it is again): both monster and maker, cause and outcome.

Impossible to unmonster myself: I ran slipshod

with beasts of the underbrush to beg and beckon. Caught my laces, stumbled along the bluffs.

GIVEN

Given a mass die-off of menhaden

Given the stench all spring

Given flies circling the houses

Given windows kept closed

Given a bridge over a tributary. You adjust to the smell, lose track of time

Given a great blue heron appearing from the phragmites, wading toward you across the mudflats

Given the thin white fish in its mouth

Given a siege of baby herons swimming into view

Given their neon-green eyes, their frantic mouths

Given two men downstream, their remote-controlled drone circling the bridge where you are standing

Given you don't know whether to stay or go. The herons. The drone. The stench

Given the dead menhaden decomposing within weeks or months

Given their bodies returning to the nutrient cycle—the mudflats abundant with them, spawning marsh elder, glasswort, cordgrass

Given the grass provides shelter for the birds

Given the drone above you, the highway behind you, the stench around you: you are still seeking shelter—

HORSESHOE CRABS

The bay brims with them:
rudder-tailed, blue-blooded,
constellating in shallows, swimming on their backs.

Yesterday, one washed up on the shore.
My husband tried to coax it back
to the ocean, but to no avail. With its tail

it moored itself to the sand, secured
from him and so many predators:

shorebirds feed on their eggs;
bulkheads break the sand where they nest;

scientists harvest their blue, blue blood,
bleeding their children from them.
Those who survive—

blue bodies
dissipating into a snow of foam—
reenter the bay bled dry, or as bait.

KRISTINA SPEAKS TO HER DAUGHTER

Did you know plants can feel pain?

They flinch when we touch them. They warn their neighbors.

After a night of drinking, I dream hibiscus swells from my fingertips, bruised to the size of wall clocks, sundials, other timepieces. Here's what I know

about dreams: you start with the things you can't have, and in the end you reach

for the one thing you can always have.

I drink to feel the earth spinning under me, watch the words fall from my mouth, a fitful rain. Who knows what seeds I've watered, what I've raised.

I meant to tell you: once, I held you when you staggered on the pier.

The wood slickened after a sudden downpour. We walked home as bay winds shook the houses.

Do you remember?

We sat inside with the power gone while the bay swallowed the streets' jagged edges. Laid the picnic blanket on the living room floor. Ate peanut butter sandwiches and played every card game you knew.

When I read to you by flashlight, my thumb and finger made a shadow like wings across the pages.

SONNET WITH A DRONE AT THE END

At the bayshore, stray cats stretch out in the street,
stare you down until you move your car.
No one admits to feeding them, though nearly
everyone does. This spring, hardly any sun.
The dogwoods flowered a month too late, then burst
in a dizzy pink haze. The cloud cover heavier each day.
My husband and I jump the guardrail and walk down
to where rocks meet sand. Our shadows together pace
in triplicate, in the crosshatch of streetlights:
two becoming three. Each step a spark
that cuts through the rain and fog. Downed branches scatter
into our path, and he guides me gently over them.
A fleet of gulls lifts off the bay, sensing dusk,
the tide's coming swell. Above us, a toy drone spirals.

EARLY SPRING, I TELL KRISTINA ABOUT THE BABY

Kristina leaves her front door open.
I spend so much time here, she forgets

to apologize for the clutter on the table,
or for her daydrinking. Not that I mind.

Days like this, she's so far gone
she barely remembers anything.
Winters, she forgets she lives here.

It's easy to forget in the dark
when you don't see the bay rising.

On everything she owns, a watermark:
a ring on the bookshelf where, carelessly, she'd placed
a mug of hot whiskey. A gray stain wrapped

around the white house. Even her shin,
where she'd rinsed a cut from the blade of the car door.

You'd drink too, she told me,
if everything of yours had washed away.
Baby or no baby.

I thought she'd be happy for me,
but my happiness now seems
a luxury—last night she dreamed,

again, about drowning in the bay.
Her history of objects already
swallowed in it: coins, stones.

An earthenware planter where, deadheading hostas,
she'd cut her finger.
Glass bottles, measuring spoons.

You can't know what it's like,
she says. She's right. The world that is dying

outside the snow-bright window
is not mine to grieve.

Not my earthenware planter,
not my watermarked house.

ULTRASOUND

Head curved downward,
two gray flecks, unblinking—
eyes?—closed. Below,
a white knot, maybe
an arm, and the vibrating core
at the center was her heart
was her heart was her heart.
Floating in apocalypse
soup—how could we know?
Little island. That night
I dreamed the rising tides
of my body. Dreamed
rain heaving into a body
of water, body that
could drown a daughter.

ICEBERG

As one crack in the ice expands,
creating hundreds of tiny

icebergs—calving, they call it—

yours was a simple drift, a breaking
away.

I imagine you floating out to sea,
then returning unrecognizable:

a pixelated photo of yourself
or poorly drawn stick figure.

Your body, a broken thing:

your second birthday, coughing up
gasoline

into your pretty cake. At six, filling
with fluid, Day-Glo veins pouring

poison into a swollen heart.
Little iceberg. Little

almost. I can see it now:
the cracks, scraps of your

floating world resurfacing.
Yes, it was better this way.

VESSELS

On the bulkhead, someone has made a line
of horseshoe crab shells, a dozen or so
in single file, facing the bay—
or at least, that's where I thought
their faces would be; in fact,
the horseshoe crab has ten eyes—
top, sides, belly—
facing, then, everywhere but
the home that did them in, and their
once-inhabitants. At some point, every vessel
has to watch its contents die:
sinking ship, vase of cut flowers,
a tumble of crows from the nest.

You died when the last
of the horseshoe crabs did. What gets me
is I didn't feel it happen.
I would have been
shopping for groceries or running
the trail behind our house when your heart
stopped beating. At your age
there would have been no pain.
Your eyes were fully formed,
though still closed, neither of us seeing the other
when they cut you from me like a paper doll,
both of us comatose, languishing
in the operating room's fluorescent light.

SENTENCE

We didn't want to sleep
but at some point had to, so
we slept on the living room floor:
less commitment than holding
each other under a sheet, and less
chance of fighting since we couldn't
face each other, and besides
upstairs was hot, and not near
the bathroom, and besides
I wasn't supposed to do stairs
after the surgery, though
I did sometimes, and besides
it didn't seem right to sleep
so close to the baby's room
so soon, or in a bed the height
a child would be if she wandered in
after a bad dream, asking for
a glass of water, or in a body
like a construction fire, charred
evidence blotted on beams
and tiles, torn roof
and smoked-out windows in its wake.

PACKING UP THE HOUSE

swear to see only what is there
      and not the child
           running up and down the stairs,

the stranger caught in photos on the wall.
      Even so, there are these wraiths:
           her phantom fingers falling

on the out-of-tune piano, a hint
      of dry leaves burning on the lawn,
           a fingerprint

on canvas the color of fog,
      as if she might be here.
           Draw a tree, and then another. Days, a travelogue.

The weeks have wings, the birches pale and husk.
      Under the shingles, cracks where the house has shed
           its white teeth. The sidewalk, leaf-littered at dusk,

cracks where a tree's root arches, lifting
      page after page. Farther down, on the beach,
           sandstorms clutching at debris. Two gulls, drifting.

PALINODE

What if my body is not an apocalypse?

Not the rising seas or the sinking city or the shifting currents of the Atlantic

Not an ocean, swallowing what we haven't begun to grieve

What if my body is another kind of water?

What if my body is not a misunderstanding

                    with the changing earth?

Not the smoke gathering above the brushfires,

                    drawing a smog-tattered cloud in all

                          the other animal clouds

Not the chemical soil in the soil of other bodies

What if my body is not a metaphor?

Not a warning cry, or the vibration of a sounding board

What if my body is not a story about pain?

What if my body is just my body,

                    tied to what it knows?

KRISTINA SPEAKS TO HER DAUGHTER

To every season, the unseasonable

Rain, snow, or heat: this November, the full Frost Moon no longer calls the frost.

Cell towers rise from the cordgrass. Factory clouds point to a hole in the sky like
a cigarette burn.

No vesper sparrow's evening song calls us to prayer; no vegetables grow
from the gray swaths of soil, the upturned roots; no vessel, from the broken
porcelain, for the gravy, turnips, corn.

The seasons unseason as flaxseed oil from a cast-iron skillet. As spices, herbs,
dull in their jars.

Do you remember?

Once, we skated on the pond. Once,
                        wet snow would fall from trees.

                    I can't remember the last time anything froze so thick.

NOVEMBER

Last night, I woke from the pain,
      settled by the window to watch the garden

          ungardening. An ache rose from my core:
      my body's faulty machinery shedding

blighted tissue, what was never meant to live.
      In the backyard, fox, possum, raccoon appear
from the tattered wood. The moon, swollen on milk-thick

      blood, a white gut bloated with hunger
          or child. Impossible, that we will raise light

      again. That with any luck, we will one day be
ancestors: a chill in the blood,
          an unseasonable wind.

TURNING

The fall belongs to you, who stirred when leaves
beamed orange and flashed against a concrete sky.

You drove me past your childhood home: its square
of grass, its plaster-cast Madonna. The rusted

water tower, the makeshift crosses there,
and in the scattered light of headlights through the fog
you could name each broken kid who tried to fly.

Timeless friend. I knew you couldn't stay.
I drew the shades, turned back the clocks to buy

more time with you: it's true, the fall belongs
to you, but winter's darkest days are mine.

KRISTINA SPEAKS OF WINTER

Cousins, four girls like stacking rings
tucked in a guest bed among too-large coats.
We slept a dim half-sleep, our dreams
pervaded by the kitchen timer, the percolator,
pieces of conversation in a language
we didn't yet understand. Hours later,
we'd be carried to our cars.

                    Sundays, we huddled in the room downstairs,
cross-legged, digging through pockets
for a stray pencil, seashell, or deck of cards. Always
we craved white paper to draw each other's faces,
sharper crayons, steadier hands.

                    The winter our grandparents got sick,
days of hospital rooms starched with fluorescent light.
Nights, furniture that folded in on itself, white and
spare: the pull-out couch, the card table. Origami
comforts. TV dinners, plastic forks. Daughter, everything
we touched, even the touch itself, would disappear.

LANDFALL

Dear daughter   given and ungiven
Dear storm converging

In my body
Every day I walked with you by the water

In the rain-soaked dark

By the blue slant of abandoned houses
Chain-link fences and beware of dog signs

Every day I walked with you
Through this town claimed by the water

Harbor of cragged remains where sails
Cast a row of half moons

On the city's doorstep

I walked with you by the water
Or what the water swallowed

Traffic cone nearly mistaken for an animal
Aimless kite wandering just above the horizon

Ragged figures shuffling past the trash heaps

Dear daughter   given and ungiven
We were the thwarted the leftovers the left behinds

In the aftermath of Sandy

We were winterers   recorders of damages
Collectors of water

Heeding a primal urge to be near the sea

Raisers of glasses
Measurers of rain   and while

The flooded streets formed a barrier

We recorded our damages in thin
Concentric rings   marked our ages

In the salt air and moonlight remains

Dear daughter   Dear nameless
Forgive me   I told myself this

Sand-sliver of a town

Was not my ruin
The water rising brushstroke by brushstroke   over

Time scales from decades to centuries

Long before your existence   or mine
Like a painting of a streetscape filling with water

Lacerations in the canvas
Gleaming like stars through the drying inks

For years, warnings that it could happen here

Spring peaked early but bore no fruit
The cherry trees had blossomed in December

Covens of blackbirds that should have flown south
Set up camp along Highway 35   Dear daughter

Living less than four feet above high tide

Every day I walked with you by the changing coastline
The eroding sands of a barrier spit

Shifting flood lines and high-water marks
A full Blood Moon   the bay like uncut glass

Forgive me   when the water appeared unchanged
I pretended this was not my ruin

Dear water   great absolver
Everything I've loved I have squandered

I will myself to look only at the ocean

And not my ruin   while every day
Somewhere a village sinks from view

Pounded hour after hour by rain and relentless wind

Every day somewhere an ice fortress dismantles
Thawed with the permafrost   every day somewhere

The ocean is in the road

Streaked with glare from unpredictable evening sun
Blue ambulance light reflected   every day someone

Wading through the wreckage

Collects plastics from the beach
Or hauls car tires out of the bay

Like a hand pushing water in a bathtub

Dear blameless   Forgive me
I pretended it was not my ruin

Dear daughter   Dear island

Seas are rising, and we are in the way

When the ocean swallows this town we'll join the ranks
Of drifters   shipwrecks

Blackfish pedaling through seaweed
Abalone dreaming at rock bottom

The sculpin   its skeletal descent
The moonfish   round and iridescent

Plunging into what everyone else kept at a wary distance

Dear daughter   everything
I touch turns liquid

The stealthy creeping outward of these creeks and channels and wetlands

Enveloped you though it was not your ruin
Dear blameless   forgive me

Afraid of being alone

When every day somewhere a shift of clouds
Or slalom of wind passes

Accompanied by rolling waves and pounding rain

Every day somewhere the floodwater breathes new currents
Spins a life of its own   every day somewhere rescuers look

For survivors in the wet rubble

Every day somewhere someone's ghost
Rows its skeleton-boat through a town

With chimneys their only guides

Dear daughter   I lose track of time
These drapes drawn shut give the illusion of night

Out of touch with the outside world

We don't know when to wake and when to sleep
Soaked as we are in artificial light

Dear daughter   if there were a place for you
Outside my ruin   you never made it

Burned-out transformers and skipping power lines

Walled us in close   the house only strengthened
In its weathered resolve

It stood for what once was: a sour reminder

Dear daughter   no
I don't get to call you daughter

To salvage what could not be replaced

I didn't carry you long enough
Hard enough

We are dealing with categories here that we don't normally see

Not a daughter
An almost

An aberration

Dear almost   given and ungiven
Every day somewhere in a doctor's office

A nightmare makes landfall

Every day somewhere in a waiting room
A girl is pictured on the local news

In grimly precise detail

The mother   claiming
The unrecognizable body

Wreckage and exponential wounds

Every day somewhere someone's absence
Pierces the chemical sky   every day somewhere

Its impact will be felt

In sick clouds over the phragmites
In sounds on the pier at night

Dear almost
Drenched in my ruin

Wind sloughs the deadwood from the pine
Untethers the city's fabric   and mine

∞

Dear almost   the fall when you died the skies
Wrung themselves out

In the wake of the destruction

I tried to convince myself
My body was not my ruin   my body

A slender barrier island between the Atlantic and an estuary

Bruised chartreuse and thistle
Muscle and cluster of vine   my body

A moon rising over the ocean

The moon   cruel mother
And you   pulled under

∞

Dear almost   How many
other hearts have stopped

As the oceans warm and expand

How many hearts did it take
To clear the land

Along this stretch of the coast

So I could grieve you in this bright
And thrumming house where

Everything is missing

No one here knows   if we did
We wouldn't be able to bear it   our fragility

The fragility of barrier islands

And what does it say that I don't
Know which I grieve harder

The floating world

Or the sinking one   the heart
That stopped in my body or the heart of

This turbulent, fast-changing planet

Forgive me   I couldn't look
Forgive me   I couldn't look away

∾

Dear almost   one thousand miles south of here
A cemetery dislodged

From the deadliest floods

A resurrection   crosses
Rise from the soil like wild grasses

Water up to the attics

Skulls   an artificial hip
Drifting

Where once were steeples   peaks of snow
Where once were hills   an archipelago

The bridge past the cemetery
Up to its eyes

Everywhere—waterlines

Dear almost
Given and ungiven

When the sea swallows our graves
When rivers breach the flood lines

Eating deeper into the city's heart

All the land that's left will be a bridge   and all the roads
If they still exist   tiny causeways like wrists

Dear almost   the cemetery's crowded
It's just as well   when I join you

Sodden and stranded

May they ash me   dilute me
But not consign me

To the singular plot
Even in death found lacking

Dear almost   every day I walk without you
By the water   I cling to the rippled edges of

This cherished geography

Given and ungiven
What does it say that I find beauty in the ruin

While others said they could not bear the sight

What does it say that when
The water appears unchanged I feel absolved

Even as wave after wave of poisoned fish
Washes up on the shore

What does it say that I pretend I am safe
Anchored by the weight of a continent

Settled in splintered heaps

Moored by the shrouds and stays of a house
That still bears Sandy's waterline

Have chosen to live with that waterline

Dear almost   it was a year
Before I could dream you into a girl   who

Grew up by the water

Whose shouting would carry
Through the salt air

Whose feet would take her
The length of the boardwalk

A ribbon of sand

In her wake   Dear almost
My body remembers you though it

Owes me nothing

In dreams I walk with you
By the water

And the pain rises   as the mosses
Rise from the snow too soon   you

No longer belong here

In this dredge where nothing else
Can grow

You no longer belong   though the water
The water   remembers

NOTES

The Natalie Diaz quote in the epigraph and the line "Apocalypse soup" in "Ultrasound" are from the poem "When the Beloved Asks, 'What Would You Do If You Woke Up and I Was a Shark?'" from her collection *When My Brother Was an Aztec*, published by Copper Canyon Press.

The Nicola Sebastian quote in the epigraph is from her essay "The Woman Who Owned the Sea," originally published by *Orion Magazine* in December 2020.

The lines "Given our bodies are just our bodies, 78 percent water" in "Given (the urgency)" and "What if my body is just my body, / tied to what it knows?" in "Palinode" are adapted from Patricia Smith's poem, "Man on the TV Say," from her collection *Blood Dazzler*, published by Coffee House Press.

The line "You cannot remove water from water" in "Wawa Poem" is from Felicia Zamora's poem, "Bodies & Water," from her collection *I Always Carry My Bones*, published by the University of Iowa Press.

Italicized lines in "Ekphrasis: Sandy" and "Landfall" are from the *New York Times*'s coverage of Superstorm Sandy, including the following:

"Documentaries Thrive in Sandy's Ruins," by John Anderson, Feb. 1, 2013.

"In Middle of a Messy Election, a Nightmare Makes Landfall," by Peter Baker, Oct. 28, 2012.

"These Wetlands Helped Stop Flooding From Sandy. Now a BJ's May Move In," by Anne Barnard, Oct. 28, 2020.

"Storm Barrels Through Region, Leaving Destructive Path," by James Barron, Oct. 29, 2012.

"After the Devastation, a Daunting Recovery," by James Barron, Oct. 30, 2012.

"When Tragedy Strikes, Come Together," by David Bornstein, Oct. 30, 2012.

"Shallow Waters and Unusual Path May Worsen the Surge," by Kenneth Chang and Henry Fountain, Oct. 28, 2012.

"Our Latest High-Water Mark," by Craig Childs, Nov. 2, 2012.

"My Jersey Shore, Now in Ruins," by Kevin Coyne, Nov. 2, 2012.

"For Adults, a Catastrophe. For Children, a Memory," by KJ Dell'Antonia, Nov. 1, 2012.

"Wind-Driven Flames Reduce Scores of Homes to Embers in Queens Enclave," by Sam Dolnick and Corey Kilgannon, Oct. 30, 2012.

"Worrying Beyond Hurricane Sandy," Editorial, Oct. 31, 2012.

"Occupy Sandy: A Movement Moves to Relief," by Alan Feuer, Nov. 9, 2012.

"The Rockaway Spirit Lives After Hurricane Sandy," by Jane Garfield Frank, Jan. 28, 2013.

"The Emotional Aftermath of Hurricane Sandy," by Judith Graham, Nov. 10, 2012.

"Dark Water: A Year After Hurricane Sandy," by Sandy Keenan, Oct. 2, 2013.

"Turning Hurricane Sandy's Scars Into Badges of Survival," by N. R. Kleinfield, Oct. 28, 2013.

"New York Is Lagging as Seas and Risks Rise, Critics Warn," by Mireya Navarro, Sept. 10, 2012.

"Sign Washed Away in Hurricane Sandy Lands on Beach in France," by Andy Newman, May 31, 2018.

"The Mayor's Barrier," by Joe Nocera, Nov. 2, 2012.

"Preparing for Hurricane Sandy Along the East Coast," by Jennifer Preston, Oct. 26, 2012.

"Major Power Failures Expected Across Northeast," by Jennifer Preston, Oct. 27, 2012.

"Lessons From Sandy, a Brewing Superstorm," by Andrew C. Revkin, Oct. 26, 2012.

"The #Frankenstorm in Climate Context," by Andrew C. Revkin, Oct. 28, 2012.

"Where Boardwalks Beckoned, a Way of Life Lies in Splinters," by Wendy Ruderman and Kate Zernike, Nov. 5, 2012.

"Asbury Park Memories," by Poh Si Teng, Dec. 13, 2012.

"A House Visited by Hurricane Sandy, Now Hosting High Jinks," by Michael Wilson, Sept. 27, 2013.

"Shore Rebuilding, Renters Go South for Summer," by Kate Zernike, March 26, 2013.

"Surfing Hurricane Sandy," by Thad Ziolkowski, Feb. 24, 2017.

ACKNOWLEDGMENTS

Thanks to Christine Stroud for her deep attention and care with this book and to the entire team at Autumn House Press for bringing it into being.

Thanks to Donika Kelly for choosing *Given* and, in doing so, providing me with this incredible opportunity.

Thanks to the editors of the following publications in which these poems first appeared, sometimes in different forms: *About Place Journal: Geographies of Justice, AGNI, Bear Review, Journal of New Jersey Poets, LEON Literary Review, Narrative Northeast, The National Poetry Review, The Offing, Permafrost Magazine, phoebe, Poet Lore, Poetry Northwest, The Shore, Sugar House Review*, and *Vinyl*.

"Apostrophe" was selected as the second-place winner of the 2022 Treehouse Climate Action Poem Prize and appeared in *Poem-a-Day* on April 30, 2022.

"Ultrasound" was published as a broadside by Broadsided Press (June 2022).

Thank you to my teachers at the MFA Program for Writers at Warren Wilson College: Kaveh Akbar, Daisy Fried, Dana Levin, and Maurice Manning, for their invaluable guidance and wisdom throughout the writing of this book. To Debra Allbery, Trish Marshall, and Caleb Whitaker, without whose patience and tireless dedication this book would have been an impossibility.

Thank you to so many teachers, friends, and guides who have given measureless time and careful attention to these poems over the years: Megan Alyse, Ariana Benson, Sean Campbell, Eric Cruz, Nora Delaney, Nicole DePolo, Melissa Green, Katrina Griffith, Yeva Johnson, George Kalogeris, Olivia Kingery, Ann Kjellberg, Mitch Manning, Sierra Nelson, Bill Pierce, Daniel Pritchard, April Purvis, Prabakar Rajan, Andi Werblin Reid, Mallory Rodenberg, James Stotts, Amber Flora Thomas, Anastasia Vassos, and Lindsey Warren. You all sustain me in every possible sense.

Thank you to the *New York Times* for their indispensable coverage of Superstorm Sandy.

Thank you to the environmental groups who are doing incredible work in and around the Raritan Bay area: the Billion Oyster Project, the Plastic Wave Project, NY/NJ Baykeeper, Save Coastal Wildlife, and countless others. I have learned so much from you.

Thank you to the authors whose books inspired and informed the writing of this one: Taneum Bambrick (*Vantage*), Sumita Chakraborty (*Arrow*), Nicole Cooley (*Breach*), Tyree Daye (*Cardinal*), Natalie Diaz (*When My Brother Was an Aztec*), Melissa Green (*The Squanicook Eclogues*), Patricia Smith (*Blood Dazzler*), and Claire Wahmanholm (*Wilder*). In addition, I would be remiss if I failed to mention *Body Toxic* by Susanne Antonetta, though my own book was mostly finished by the time I read it. *Body Toxic* is essential reading for anyone looking to understand the history of environmental disaster at the Jersey Shore and its effects on individuals and communities. I am immensely grateful to Antonetta, and to Doug Carlson for introducing me to her work.

Thank you to my therapist, Dr. Christiane Manzella, who has pulled me out of the wreck time and time again.

Thank you to my parents, Lori and David Katz, and to my sister, Emily Katz Jaeger, and her husband, Joseph Jaeger, and to more friends and relatives than I can possibly name here for their endless support and for showing up no matter what. You are all on my mind and heart, when I write and always.

And finally, thank you to Christian Duncan, my partner in love, in loss, and in life. You have never, ever stopped believing in me. I love you.

NEW AND FORTHCOMING FROM AUTUMN HOUSE PRESS

The Scorpion's Question Mark by J. D. Debris
Winner of the 2022 Donald Justice Poetry Prize, selected by Cornelius Eady

Ishmael Mask by Charles Kell

Origami Dogs: Stories by Noley Reid

Taking to Water by Jennifer Conlon
Winner of the 2022 Autumn House Poetry Prize, selected by Carl Phillips

Discordant by Richard Hamilton
Winner of the 2022 CAAPP Book Prize, selected by Evie Shockley

The Neorealist in Winter: Stories by Salvatore Pane
Winner of the 2022 Autumn House Fiction Prize, selected by Venita Blackburn

Otherwise: Essays by Julie Marie Wade
Winner of the 2022 Autumn House Nonfiction Prize, selected by Lia Purpura